I Still Loved You

Hetvi Shah

You kissed me like a last breath,
Now I spend my entire life exhaling you

Feel it all, just like the love you have always known.

Dear You,

If you're holding this, I already know.
You're tired. Maybe not just from the day but from
feeling this much for this long.
You've loved someone who didn't love you back the
way you needed or maybe they did but not enough to
stay.This isn't some neat story with blame or clean
endings. It's messy. I was messy. He was too. I ended
things when I should've chosen him, chosen us over my
fears. I waited for texts that never came. I answered
calls I
should've ignored. I took him back when I knew better. I
broke it. He broke it. We both did. I kept looking for him in
people who weren't him. I married someone else just to
feel chosen.
But god, I never stopped loving him. Even after all this years
through silence, distance, even if we are nothing. I wrote this
when he left me on seen, between therapy sessions and more
after too many goodbyes. I wrote to forget him but every
word brought me closer.
And here's what I learned: love doesn't vanish. It stays in
every corner of your heart, even when the story is messy
and unfinished. Life's too short for regrets, for love left
unsaid, for apologies you never spoke. So if you're still
carrying someone like I was, read on.
Not for closure, but so you know you're not the only one
who loved someone that much and still had to walk away.

With everything I couldn't say
The Girl Who Still Loved Him Anyway

It took a second to match but a lifetime isn't enough to unmatch from my bones.

I didn't go looking for you or for this. Not when I swiped right, not in a person. But it found me. *Us*. It was inevitable. Like we were always destined to be. Like the universe had been waiting to hand you over all along.

I've met so many people, their faces blurring into a sea
of forgotten names.
But your eyes stand out, like they've *known* mine in
another life, another time.
Black, deep and endless,
but the way they hold mine, as if we've shared secrets
in a world we can't quite remember.
As if we've loved before, lost before,
and found each other again,
just to feel that familiar ache.

My world narrowed to the size of his smile and I was content to let it.

Your smile felt like *gravity*,
and I was tired of floating.

I played the fool, got every answer wrong,
hoping you'd see through it all along.
I knew the truth, but let it slip,
so you'd kiss me and close the gap between our lips.
I wish you'd known I lost on purpose,
just to feel, the warmth of your touch,
the love so real.
I *wanted* you close, but never knew how to say,
that losing was the only way I knew to make you stay.

I don't remember falling in love with you — only that one day, I already was.

I don't know when I fell in love with you. There was no clear moment, no spark that announced itself. We just kept meeting again and again like the world quietly conspired to make space for us.

Your hand found mine one day, without a word, without asking. You didn't need to. It felt like you already knew it belonged there.

And maybe that was it. Or maybe it was all the little moments before and after, layering softly, until love was just... there.

Some nights, with you I couldn't tell if I was falling asleep or falling for you.

Maybe I still can't.

I was so used to hiding that I forgot what it felt like to be found.

It feels like breathing for the first time. Like someone finally sees all the messy, tangled parts of me and instead of turning away, he stays. He looks right through the walls I've built and somehow, he still loves what's behind them.

With him, I don't have to hide or shrink. I can just *be* and that's enough. It's terrifying and it's the safest I've ever felt.

You said you believed in destiny, then vanished like mist.

I watched you leave from city to city, wrote poems when you didn't to reply. I kissed my phone at midnight no one kissed back.

Long distance never scared me only your silence di

You didn't leave. You just responded slower. Stopped asking how my day was. Stopped noticing when I didn't tell you. I kept holding space for you, while you shrank into the distance between us. That's the thing about loss, it doesn't always come crashing down. Sometimes it's just the *growing* quiet between heartbeats.

I left before you could leave because I knew you'd forget to say goodbye.

I was still writing poems while you were rewriting your future without me in it.

You didn't break my heart. You forgot you were holding it.

Every breath became a reminder of the one I couldn't take with him.

The world's lost its color,
everything feels so still,
even the sun seems colder,
like it's lost its will.

Some people are like seasons, they come and change everything and slowly start to leave.

We met in spring, loved through summer, fell apart in autumn and now winter feels like a lifetime of *waiting* for something that's already gone.

I deserve the kind of love that doesn't leave me questioning if I'm enough.

The kind that doesn't leave me staring at my phone, waiting for a text that never comes. The kind that holds me like I'm fragile, not like I'm temporary. I deserve love that *stays* not just in words, but in the quiet, in the ordinary, in the way your hand finds mine without thinking. Love that doesn't make me feel like an option. Love that *chooses me*, every single day, even when it's hard.

You know what's sacred? The friend who shows up with sweatpants and ice cream when you're drowning in post-breakup tears. Not the fancy kind who says "I told you so," but the one who sits in your mess with you, who lets you ruin their good shirt with your mascara stains. These are the people who love you in *present tense* when your heart's stuck in the past. Funny how heartbreak gives you the sharpest vision and suddenly you see exactly whose hands are *steady* enough to hold your broken parts.

I told myself maybe this time, we'd learn how to love better.

Can we meet? you asked.
I said no, my voice barely holding,
hands shaking with memories I never meant to
keep.
But my feet moved on their own,
betraying all the silence I'd built.

And there you were,
unchanged in the way only memory allows
as if time had spared you.
But it hadn't. Not really.
Not for me.

So much time has passed.
Too much.
And though I stood in front of you,
I was already gone
just a loner passing through
the ruins of something
I once called home.

You asked to restart what you never finished.

You said "let's be us again"
like *we* hadn't once ended
with tear-stained goodbyes.

I said yes, but I didn't tell you I was scared to love again.

Hope is such a beautiful liar.
I held its hand while ignoring the wounds still bleeding.

*And still, I chose you, even knowing how easily we
break.*

Time took you from me but it also led me back to you.

Falling in love with you again feels like breathing after forgetting how.

The first time, it was this fire all new, wild and full of unspoken promises. I loved you with everything I didn't yet know how to protect. And when we lost it, I thought that was the end of the story. I grieved you like a chapter I'd never get back.

But then life, in its quiet way, brought you to me again. Not as you were, not as I was but somehow, still *us*. And this time, it's different. I don't love you blindly anymore. I love you *because* I've seen what it's like to lose you. I love you with both hands open but holding on like a prayer.

This time, I don't need fireworks. Just your hand in mine, steady and real. I hold this love sacred now not because it's perfect, but because we survived enough to find it again.

And I won't let go. Not again.

Slow dances are where time stops and hearts find their rhythm.

Where time forgets to move,
where hands speak louder than words,
and hearts, for a moment, beat in the same quiet rhythm.
Nothing else matters in that moment.

We were strangers to the city but not to each other.

His hoodie shields me,
Laughter warms up the cold night,
Bike traces unknown paths
In the city's empty streets,
We are lost, yet *found* in love.

I hate how far you are and I love you anyway.

Some days, the distance feels unbearable like I'm holding my breath, waiting for you. I miss your voice, your warmth, the way the world feels softer when you're near. It hurts, this kind of missing. It sits heavy in my chest, sharp and tender all at once. But even through the ache, I *choose* you. In every moment, in every mile between us, it's still you. *Always*.

You left, but the fear of abandonment stayed, like a ghost I can't escape.

We've loved, we've broken, we've come back together,
but one thing never changed: the fear. The fear that one
day, you'd walk *away* and never look back. And you did.
But what you didn't take with you was the
fear. It's still here, haunting me, whispering that
everyone I love will leave. You taught me how to love
but not enough to take away my fear.

Choosing peace over pain, even when it costs you pieces of yourself.

You forgive people not because you forget how they hurt you, but because the thought of losing them entirely feels like losing a part of yourself. You hold on, even when the weight of their silence or the sting of their actions cuts deep. You tell yourself it's worth it, that their presence, however fractured, is better than the emptiness of their absence.

I want to be the reason your camera roll is full of sunsets and your heart is full of me.

I want to be the one you think of when the sky burns orange and pink, when the sun dips low and the world feels still. I want to be the name that whispers in your mind as you raise your phone, capturing a moment too beautiful to keep to yourself. I want to be the person you *wish* were there, standing beside you, sharing the quiet awe of a fading day. Not because I need to be remembered but because I want to be the one who makes those fleeting moments feel eternal. I want to be the one you miss, even when the world is beautiful because without me, it's just a little less whole.

I gave you my heart but you handed it back like it was a word you didn't understand.

Maybe I said *I love you* too soon.
Too much, too fast, too full of hope.
And your silence it was louder than any no.
Some of us speak love like a *promise*,
believing it will be held gently,
but not everyone knows what to do with a heart placed in
their hands.

You treated my heart like a part-time job.

I became something you only needed when it was *convenient*, a brief escape from your world. I tried to stay, to make myself matter but you kept pushing me away, like I was nothing more than a distraction. I was there in your spare moments, clinging to whatever scraps you gave me, but I was never really a part of you.

I gave you everything and you still couldn't see me.

I think I *misunderstood* love. I gave everything, even when it drained me. I thought love was being the first thought in the morning, being the one they couldn't wait to see. I thought love was whispered prayers, poems written in your name, a bond that held strong. But I was wrong. I loved too much and it was never enough. I was always the one reaching, always the one caring, while you stayed distant, untouched. I thought if I gave more, I'd be seen, I'd be *chosen*. But I was never your first thought, never the one you held close. I gave my heart away, but I never got yours in return. Now, I'm left with nothing but the emptiness of loving someone who took everything from me, who slowly ripped my heart apart without ever feeling it breaking.

I didn't want to be a pause. I wanted to be a priority

I wasn't asking to be your world,
Just something you didn't put on hold.

We believed we were the exception until silence proved us wrong.

He told me about the way distance ruins things.
How it starts small with missed calls, tired replies and
ends in silence.
I looked him in the eyes and swore we'd be the
exception.
But belief isn't armor.
And now I see.
Even the strongest hearts
Can break quietly, from far away.

Before you break me again, let me choose the ending.

I kept falling for you and each time, it was with the same
hope, the same love only for distance to stretch its cold
fingers between us. I tried to hold on, to believe that love
could bridge the miles that we could make it work but
somewhere along the way, I started to disappear waiting
for a call that never came, staring at screens that couldn't
feel like touch. The silence grew louder and my heart,
once full of you, began to ache with the weight of it all.
I'm not *giving up* on love, not on you but on the distance
that's slowly pulling us apart, leaving me miserable in a
place where love can no longer live. So let me choose
the ending. Let me walk away before you do, because
it's better this way.

You didn't choose someone else, you just never chose me loud enough.

You didn't choose someone else, you just never chose me loud enough.

I wasn't competing with another girl. I was competing with your ambition, your silence and your unread messages. And when I finally left, it wasn't because I
stopped loving you. It was because I got *tired* of proving I was worth loving back.

You took your warmth; the world kept the winter.

The world is sharp
without your hands.
Diamonds dim,
the moon wears your face
too bright to bear,
too far to reach.

I loved you in a way that words could never reach and you'll never know that.

You'll never truly know what you meant to me not in the way I felt you, not in how effortlessly you became a part of me. I could never find the right words to explain how *your* presence made me feel whole, like something missing had quietly returned. You'll never understand how deeply you held my heart, how much love I carried for you in silence. And maybe that's how it was meant to be. Somethings are meant to be felt not explained.

You touched me like you wanted to stay, then left like you never did.

Your hands promised forever. Your
feet knew the way out.
I mistook heat for love.

Desire is not devotion, I learned that late.

Love is strange, it gives you everything you need and then takes it all away.

You were my safe place,
and the storm that shattered it.
You were my home,
and the reason I felt homeless.
You were my solution,
and my problem,
and I loved you anyway,
because how could I not?
You were *everything*, all at once.

We don't just grieve what we lost. We grieve what we never had the chance to hold.

It's not the memories that hurt,
it's the lack of them.
The photos we never took,
the red dress I never wore for you.
Everything whispering what could have been.
How do you mourn something that never happened?
How do you grieve a future that lived only in your mind,
a love that never got the *chance* to breathe, to bloom, to
be?

I waited for the universe to forget your name. It never did.

No matter where I went, your name found me, tucked into clouds, in street signs, written into every passing moment.

Maybe the universe wasn't showing me you
maybe it was showing me I still wasn't over you.

We don't get to erase people just because we are no longer theirs to hold.

I regret walking away so completely.
I told myself it was easier for both of us if I just
disappeared.
But the truth is, I was *afraid*. Afraid of seeing you move
on,
afraid that if I stayed in your life even a little,
I'd never really let go.
So I cut you out like a coward, pretending it was
strength.
But love doesn't vanish when we demand it to,
it stays.
I miss you and I owe you this confession: I was wrong.
Wrong to think I could unlove you neatly. Wrong to
believe absence would hurt less than longing.

When the heart breaks, the body seeks other ways to feel.

After we ended, I tried to feel *anything* but the pain you left behind. I climbed mountains, jumped from bridges, buried needles in my skin as if physical pain could *outrun* the emotional ache. But pain doesn't leave just because you're brave. It stays a quiet shadow until you learn to carry it without breaking.

Sometimes, the bravest thing is to let the pain stay until it no longer hurts.

My body remembers you better than my heart does.

Even now, my skin hums where you touched me. The curve of my waist, the dip of my collarbone, they still ache for your hands. I scrub myself raw in the shower but I can't wash you away. Because some marks aren't visible. They're just felt, long after you're gone.

The rain falls now just like you always wanted but it doesn't feel romantic. It feels like the sky is crying for us

I stand in it, soaked,
but it doesn't feel like a dream.
It feels like the sky knows we're gone
that we never held each other in it,
never *danced* in the downpour
like a scene straight out of a movie,
where every drop is a step toward something magical.
I feel the weight of every drop,
each one like an *apology* from the heavens,
for the moments we missed,
for the love we let fade into the silence.
If only we had let the rain guide us,
if only we had danced under it instead of walking away.

*I don't even want him back—I just want back the version
of me who believed in us.*

The girl who laughed at his texts.
Who believed love could fix what was broken.
She wore hope like perfume always light, constant,
everywhere she went.
She was fearless.
Now she's afraid of saying too much, of feeling too
deeply.
Anxiety lives in her chest now, so she travels not to just
explore but to escape.
The girl who once ran toward love now walks away
from anything that feels like it.
She used to wear her heart on her sleeve. Now I wear
silence like armour.

*Losing them is one thing. Losing who you were with
them is another*

I tried to replace you with someone warmer.

Their hands were kinder but didn't know where I'm ticklish. Kisses more careful but lacking your specific hunger. You ruined me for half-love, for almost-right. Now I sleep alone, waiting for either your return or my standards to lower.

Every time I left, I hoped you'd chase me.

You never did.
Maybe that's why I kept leaving to be proven wrong.

Some hearts break themselves trying to be chosen.

I walked away, not because I stopped loving but because I started needing.

Needing isn't weakness,
it's just love.
Asking for a return trip.

Because love can't wait forever in a place only one heart shows up.

Forgetting you took longer than having you.

I counted the days we had,
but I spent even more counting the days I've been
without.
Each minute was a reminder of the moments I never
thought I'd lose.
I thought I'd get over you, but each step away from you
felt like I was walking further into the dark.
And now I wonder, if forgetting you is the price I have
to pay for loving you.

*Choosing someone because they're there is not the same
as choosing them because they're you.*

I tried to *replace* you, to fill the space you left with new experiences. Dates, conversations and kisses they were all attempts to find a way out of the pain.
But each time I found myself coming back to you, to the realization that no one else could make me feel the way you did. So I sought a stable life, a *convenient* life: Marriage.

A decision made in the absence of your presence.

I said yes to a man who stayed.

He held out his hand
and I said yes out of need, not forgetting you.

Some vows are made in the absence of closure.

You were my lobster, the one I thought I'd grow with, claw in claw.

A silly reference, something I picked up from a show. But it felt right, like you are the one I am meant to hold onto, through every twist and turn of life. Lobsters mate for life, they find their partner and stay, no matter what. That's what I want with you, a love that weathered *every tide, every season, every storm.*

You didn't lose me, I buried myself in someone else just to forget you.

I knew it would hurt you if I married someone else. Maybe that was part of it. Maybe I thought your pain would finally prove I meant something. I wanted your attention not because I stopped loving you, but because I never did. I wanted a reaction, a sign that you still cared, that I hadn't imagined it all.

But in trying to make you feel something, I forgot what I was risking. I was so focused on being seen by you that I didn't see what I was doing to us. I thought I was making a move but really, I was making a mistake. Because the moment I said yes to someone else, I quietly said no to us.

And I didn't realize that until it was too late.

Drunk texts are just sober truths wearing liquid courage.

I sip my third whiskey sour and keep tracing the rim like it's the *edge* of my self-control. You should see how carefully I type, thumbs moving slow as grief, autocorrect fighting my heart's messy handwriting. These messages always start with "Remember when-" as if either of us could ever forget. The bubbles appear then disappear and I'm left staring at my own reflection in the black mirror of read receipts. I delete the evidence by morning but we both know the words were real.

Some lines, once crossed, can never be redrawn.

We can never be friends. Not after the way your lips traced mine, not after the way your breath became my air. Friends don't know the weight of each other's silence, the heat of each other's touch, the way a single glance can reveal everything.

We crossed a line, one that can't be uncrossed. And now, every word, every laugh, every shared moment feels like a betrayal of what we were.

Friends don't ache for each other in the quiet hours of the night. Friends don't remember the way their skin felt under trembling hands.

So no, we can't be friends. Because friends don't know the taste of each other's lips— *and I'll never forget yours*

I watched you smoke, wondering if it was my kiss you missed.

Across the table, your eyes locked mine,
but your fingers curled around her.
I watched as it rested between your lips,
wondering if you smoked because it was the only way
you could still *feel* something, something close,
something warm, as if your lips were still touching mine.
If I were that cigarette, would you hold me like that
again? Would you bring me close, let me burn, just so
you could feel me near, even if only for a moment?
But I'm just a girl, sitting here, watching you slip away,
one exhale at a time.
I wish I could be something you'd hold like that, just
once more, to feel your lips on mine again.

I didn't ask if you were seeing someone, because I wasn't ready to die that way.

I wasn't prepared to crumble under the weight of your answer, to have everything between us broken into a thousand pieces. It wasn't curiosity that held me back it was fear. Fear that the truth would come too sharp, too final and I'd have no *choice* but to swallow it whole. So I kept my silence, hoping the question would stay buried, untouched and safe.

I know you heard my heart that night, just like I heard yours, beating in time with love that didn't need to be spoken.

You never used the L word, but in the way you moved
like the world was a storm and I was the only shelter you
needed.
You pulled me in, our breaths tangled hearts pounding in
a rhythm so fierce, it felt like my lips might break.
And they did, under yours, a kiss that answered every
unspoken craving, every hunger I never knew I had.
Your eyes, holding me like I was precious, like you were
terrified to let go.
We melted together, skin to skin as if we were never
meant to be two *separate* beings.
Your fingers tracing mine as if you were claiming every
broken piece.
In your arms, I was whole, my flaws vanished into
nothing, as if they never existed.
Your touch spoke a language I only understood in the
deepest parts of me. If this isn't love, then tell me, what
is? This fire, this closeness, just us, tangled in something
too vast to name, too fragile to hold.

We didn't make love, we said goodbye it in sweat and silence.

You said, "Let's not complicate."
But how do I simplify a love that lived in every corner of
me?
You said you wanted the present. And I realized, my gift
was *always* the future.

I never had the words to tell him that I'm still holding on to you.

The last time we met, I wish I had told you that I'm still not over you that I still love you, and no matter how much I try, I can't unlove you.
I wish I could've told you how *painful* it is to love you and yet I carry it with me even now. Life's too short for regrets but here I am, holding on to all of this, too scared to speak it.
One day, I'll have the courage to tell you everything I can't seem to let go of.

We chase after so many things in life, but the rarest of all is finding someone who feels like home.

We all search for a place to belong and sometimes, that place is a person. If, by some miracle, you find that person the one who makes your soul feel like it's *finally* come home, hold on tight. Don't let them slip away. You'll recognize them, I promise. It won't be fireworks and grand gestures all the time, but a quiet, steady warmth, a sense of belonging you've never known before. And if, for some foolish reason, you decide to shatter that feeling, to walk away, remember this: love and hate are two sides of the same coin. The pain you unleash, the emptiness you create, it won't stay contained. It will *boomerang*, find its way back to you. You'll understand, then, the coldness of the space you left behind. You'll feel the weight of what you destroyed. And trust me, rebuilding that home, that sense of belonging is a long, lonely road. So, please, if you're lucky enough to find *that* person, hold on tight. Cherish them. Protect them. Build a *life* with them.

Every now and then, I check your socials, like it'll bring you back.

I still check your socials, even though I know it's pointless. It's like I'm searching for something that will make me feel *close* to you again, even if just for a moment. I read through our old messages, each word bringing back a flood of memories and I wonder if you ever do the same. Maybe you don't, maybe you've already moved on. But I can't stop. It's like I'm holding on to the last thread of something that's already slipping away. And each time I check, each time I read, it hurts, but I can't seem to let it go.

Cities can be soulmates too.

These streets hold my growth and grief. The skyline greets me like an old lover whenever I come home.

*Will my name ever escape your lips, or am I a secret
you've buried too deep.*

When you tell your story, the one about your life, your
journey, the people you love, will I be in it? Will *us* be a
mention? Will there be a pause, a footnote, a mention of
me?
Or will I be a blank page, a skipped paragraph, a
character lost in the *crowd* of your memories? Like I
never mattered at all.

Our kisses tasted like memory, not hope.

Each kiss screaming wildly: I missed you,
but never, I won't leave again.

Hope is the cruelest thing we carry.

I still wait for your text. Still pause at songs that remind
me of you. Hope is the last leaf clinging to a winter tree,
refusing to let go even when the wind screams it's over.
I wonder when I'll stop expecting you to come back.
Maybe never

We keep circling back like chapters of a favourite book.

No matter how far I turn the pages,
A part of me always finds its way back to you
like a dog-eared corner, worn soft from all the rereading.
Maybe it's muscle memory, maybe its madness.
But loving you feels like reciting a line I know by heart
even when it hurts.
Even when I promised I wouldn't flip back.
There's *comfort* in familiarity, even if the ending never
changes.
Maybe we weren't meant to be the final chapter just the
one I can't stop revisiting.

We needed to break to learn how to bend.

Nine years later, your touch still feels like *home*. They say our cells regenerates every seven years and yet somehow, you never faded from mine. I've worn other hands, other arms but none ever felt quite right. It's like my body kept the memory of you beneath the surface, in the places that science can't reach.

We had to break to learn how not to. To learn what it meant to hold. Love, back then, was all fire and ache. Now, it's quieter. Less perfect. More real. We don't stay because it's easy. We stay because we *choose* to. And in this messy, deliberate choosing there's a kind of love I will never know how to name.

What if I told you that falling isn't failing, it's just letting someone catch you?

When you're too tired from building the life you dreamed of, when your hands ache and your heart feels heavy, I hope you know this:

You can fall.

You can fall into my arms and I'll hold you without a word of judgment. I'll tell you its okay to be this tired, this broken, this human. I'll remind you that even the strongest trees bend in the storm and the most beautiful stars burn themselves out to shine.

You don't have to carry it all alone. That I am here, *if* you'll let me be.

The moon knows I *lied*. I told everyone I moved on, that I don't think of you. But each night, I sit under its glow and feel the weight of everything unsaid. The goodbye that never felt real. The love that never fully left.

I had a pattern of quitting, but I always called it protecting myself.

I walked away before I could be left again.
I thought I was brave
but maybe I was just scared of being chosen
and then forgotten.
Now I sit with the truth: I never gave love a full chance
because I never believed I was worth staying for.

Sometimes, we abandon love before it has the chance to abandon us.

I'm tired of healing. Tired of becoming.

They always say you'll be stronger, better, whole.
But no one talks about the days you just want to stop
feeling everything.
Not better.
Not stronger.
Just quiet.
Just untouched.

I would know you by touch alone, even if the world forgot your name.

Your hands. I still see the lines, those long, strange fingers *woven* with mine. It's carved in me, a map I'd follow anywhere. Even across lifetimes. If we meet again, I'll know it's you in a heartbeat.

Some losses don't heal, they just become the quiet ache
you carry in your bones.

You know how they say time heals? It's a *lie*, really. Time doesn't erase the pain. It just lets you wear it differently. It's not about forgetting. It's about remembering something beautiful, even though it couldn't stay. It's a part of me now and maybe, a part of you too, if you've ever loved something that slipped away.

Sometimes, the most painful things are the ones we never speak.

Another May arrives and with it, your day but my heart remembers. I don't say Happy Birthday, not from bitterness, but because my love has learned to stay quiet. I carry you in silence, with both pain and pride, letting the quiet speak what words never could.

I made you the excuse, but deep down, I knew I was the reason all along.

I needed someone to *blame*, someone to carry the weight of my mistakes. You were easy to point to, easy to say, "It's your fault" when all along, it was also mine to carry. I hid behind you because facing what I'd done felt too hard. I told myself it was easier to make you the problem but deep down, I knew the truth: I was the one who had let things *fall apart*.

This is how it ends, with a star loving her moon from afar.

I still wear you near my heart in ink,
in memory, in all the ways I never said goodbye.
You were never mine to keep.
But always mine to feel.

They say life flashes before your eyes in the end and only minutes to remember, I'll save you for last. I'll let your memory be the final breath I take, the one that carries me into whatever comes next. And in that moment, I hope you know that I'm holding onto *you* as I let go of everything else.

If I die before you miss me, would you still feel it?

I hope when I'm gone,
you *pretend* you loved me
the way I pretended you already did.

Some goodbyes aren't endings, they're just pauses in a story that isn't finished yet.

There's a part of me that believes we'll meet again.
That one day, the universe will bring us back to the same place,
to have the conversation we needed to have.
The one where words don't fail,
where silence between us fade.
I imagine it your eyes meeting mine, not with regret but with understanding. A quiet *acceptance* of all that was, and all that could have been.

I didn't know how much I loved you until I couldn't say it anymore.

And isn't that always how it goes?
We learn the weight of what we lost only after it's too
late to hold it.

Maybe you weren't distant to hurt me. Maybe you were just overwhelmed by the weight of becoming.

I see it now, how you were trying to become someone
new, someone better, even if it meant stepping away
from everything familiar. I didn't understand that at the
time but now I do. You weren't pulling away to hurt me,
you were just trying to *survive* your own transformation.
And it breaks my heart to know how much you carried
alone, when all I wanted was to be there with you.

I hope you find a love where words aren't needed to understand each other.

I hope you find a love that listens to you without you needing to say a word, like when you're making coffee in the morning and they just know the right moment to hand you the cup, warm and ready, without asking. Or when you're quiet after a long day and they sit beside you, letting the silence speak for itself, understanding exactly what you need. A love that notices the small things, how your shoulders tense when you're stressed, or how you laugh a little too loudly when you're nervous and knows how to ease them without a single question. I hope you find that, because it's in those everyday moments, the ones where words aren't necessary, that true understanding grows.

I hope when love finds me again, I am brave enough to let it in, heart wide open and unafraid.

I hope that when love finds me again, I am ready to feel it all the highs that make my heart race and the lows that remind me how deeply I'm capable of caring. I want to feel every laugh, every touch, every quiet moment in its purest form, without *fear* of the intensity. I hope I've learned that vulnerability isn't weakness but strength and I am ready to surrender to it fully. I want to experience love without holding back, to embrace the beauty of it even when it's messy, even when it's complicated. No more half-hearted attempts or *guarded* emotions when love finds me again, I want to feel every bit of it, raw and unfiltered, as if for the first time.

If you've ever loved someone you couldn't keep, you know that love doesn't disappear just because life pulls you apart.

Some hearts stay quietly woven into yours, not to be
held but to be remembered, *always*.

Maybe, in another life, we'll find the love we couldn't keep.

But in this one, we're just a story that ended too soon.

Loved. Lost. Learned.

If any line made you pause, feel or reminded you of your own story, slide into my DMs @Istilllovedyou.book I'd love to know which words found their way to you.